i, nemophile

# i, nemophile

POEMS

allie picketts

All poems copyright © 2023, Allie Picketts

No part of this book may be reproduced in any form by any means without the express permission of the author. This includes reprints, excerpts, photocopying, recording, photographing, or any future means of reproducing text. If you would like to do any of the above, please seek permission first by contacting the author, who will be happy to hear from you and will likely say yes.

Contact: allie.piano@protonmail.com
www.alliepickettswrites.com

ISBN: 978-1-7380951-0-0 (softcover)
ISBN: 978-1-7380951-1-7 (eBook)

Edited by Susan Musgrave/susanmusgrave.com

Cover photos by Belinda White/applestarphoto.com

Cover photo-illustration by Jan Westendorp
Cover and book design by Jan Westendorp/katodesignandphoto.ca

Printed and bound in Canada by
Island Blue Printorium Bookworks, Victoria, BC

# Contents

| | |
|---|---|
| WITH THANKS TO | ix |
| ABOUT THIS BOOK | xi |
| WHERE CREDIT IS DUE | xiii |
| PLACE NAMES | xv |
| | |
| away | 1 |

## I. Spring

| | |
|---|---|
| Moss | 5 |
| the honey-sweet earth | 6 |
| Spring break, Quadra Island | 7 |
| there are still birds here | 8 |
| Oceansong | 9 |
| Earthsong | 10 |
| This little light | 12 |
| Ar Hyd y Nos | 13 |
| to think of a tree | 14 |
| it must have been the onions | 15 |
| Commendation | 17 |
| cheers | 18 |
| born this way | 19 |
| míqən | 21 |
| sooner or later | 22 |

## II. Summer

| | |
|---|---|
| In which there are at least four miracles at SELEK̓TEȽ | 27 |
| water and I | 29 |
| melon/begin | 30 |
| Brimming Moon Dream | 31 |
| Wilderness | 33 |
| light, and momentary troubles | 35 |
| the world gives me | 36 |
| ʔAdaits$\underline{x}$ in August 2021 | 37 |
| unpolished | 38 |
| tell me | 39 |
| Arbutus | 40 |
| the echo of leaving | 41 |
| Bike | 42 |
| All recycled materials | 44 |
| god apology | 45 |

## III. Autumn

| | |
|---|---:|
| i, nemophile | 49 |
| who | 50 |
| Summerland | 51 |
| Someday witch | 53 |
| Windsong | 54 |
| Thirsty | 55 |
| In which the fish teach philosophy at SELEKTEL | 56 |
| Ides of November | 57 |
| peace | 59 |
| Shall I go? | 60 |
| getting somewhere | 61 |
| Hedgerow | 62 |
| Air | 63 |
| G.P. | 64 |

## IV. Winter

| | |
|---|---|
| Doorway | 67 |
| Owlmas | 68 |
| Windows | 69 |
| *Another storm comin'* | 70 |
| Drawn | 71 |
| December medicine | 72 |
| Odd | 73 |
| Lines on the shortest day | 74 |
| Gardening in January | 75 |
| Point No Point | 76 |
| thy neighbour's chimes | 77 |
| The waiting-time | 78 |
| Magellan Quay | 79 |
| It is February | 80 |
| once was lost | 81 |
| Remembering blue | 82 |

## with thanks to

my grandparents and parents, sisters and children

Smiler, Heather, Niki, Shelby, and Kaitlyn

Jan Zwicky: for thinking my poems worth reading

Susan Musgrave: for suggestions that much improved them

Bruce Vogt: for a great number of things

Jan Westendorp: for incredible design expertise and endless patience

the Sooke Writers' Collective, particularly Deb Clay, Dóni Eve, Fatima-Ayan Malika Hirsi, and Clare Winstanley

all those who write, say, sing, and play things that make my heart explode

and a very large number of inspiring people mostly located in (but not limited to) Delta, Surrey, Victoria, Sooke, and Cayman.

## about this book

With the exception of 'Magellan Quay', these poems were written on and inspired by the life-giving lands of Kwakwa̱ka̱'wakw, Nuu-chah-nulth, and Coast Salish Peoples. I am thankful and humbled to live and write in T'Sou-ke territory.

I am a descendant of uninvited settlers who stole land and way of life from the inhabitants of this place. My culture and its systems continue to do incredible harm to the land and its Peoples. Because of this, and because I am in a position of privilege when it comes to race, class, and education, I know I have a lot to learn about the ways in which I am causing harm. I have done my best in this book, but learning is never finished, and I want to sincerely apologize for any harm I may cause.

I also want to acknowledge that, despite the strength of my love for nature, I will never understand the depth of connection with this land experienced by those whose ancestors have lived here sustainably and in harmony with the other-than-human world for millennia.

I use the original names of several locations mentioned in these poems with respect and in an attempt to bring some small awareness to how much colonization has shaped our senses of place and land 'ownership'.

Wherever I have gone, I have been a guest, and I try to tread as lightly as I can. All my gratitude to those who tend and protect the Earth.

The typeface in the poems' body is Macklin Text, part of a contemporary super-family designed by Malou Verlomme. It is a modern interpretation of early 19th-century typeface designs, particularly those by Vincent Figgins, whose typefaces were a response to the rapid social changes brought by the Industrial Revolution.

## where credit is due

'Moss', 'Hedgerow' and 'Windows' were previously published in the Vancouver Island Regional Library's *Sea & Cedar* Literature and Art Magazine, 22 August, 2023.

A previous version of 'Shall I go?' was published electronically as a Poetry Pause by the League of Canadian Poets, 16 June, 2022.

'The waiting-time' and 'All recycled materials' were previously published in *Sooke Roots*, Anthology Nine of the Sooke Writers' Collective, 2022.

'Brimming Moon Dream' and 'Windsong' were previously published in *Where We Reside: Poems of Time and Place, 11 Sooke Poets Reflect*, 2022.

'Remembering blue' was originally published by the Sooke Region Literacy Project and the Vancouver Island Regional Library (Sooke branch) as part of the Sooke Poetry Walk, April 2022.

## place names

ʔAdaits<u>x</u> (diitiidʔaaʔt<u>x</u>), also known as Fairy Creek, is on Pacheedaht territory.

míqən (lək̓ʷəŋiʔnəŋ), also known as Beacon Hill, is on lək̓ʷəŋən territory.

PKOLS (SENĆOŦEN), also known as Mount Douglas, is on W̱SÁNEĆ territory.

SELEKTEŁ (SENĆOŦEN), also known as Goldstream, is on W̱SÁNEĆ territory.

*Go out in the woods, go out. If you don't go out in the woods, nothing will ever happen and your life will never begin.*

from 'The Wolf's Eyelash' by Clarissa Pinkola Estés, copyright © 1970, from *Rowing Songs for the Night Sea Journey: Contemporary Chants* (privately published, 1989)

## away

I fell away in the forest
and no one heard. at least, not at first,
though when they did, they staged a protest.
but my insides were bigger
than their outsides, so I won. inasmuch
as one can win while losing, apparently,
everything.

# I. Spring

## Moss

I can't tell you, but you will know,
        if you have scaled an at-times stream and tried
        to match the water-trickling tune with your unwieldy voice,
and didn't feel it leave but noticed at last
        that the pain in your throat had gone.

I think the moss absorbed it or it rose to
        the ancient branches and was caught there while you
        escaped to home, but some of the forest stayed in your feet,
so that night you grew roots and drew from the earth
        until you could hold no more.

Be gentle with yourself:
you are not wrong for walking on the moss.

## the honey-sweet earth

a piece of paper that I lost
on which was written
*the honey-sweet earth,*
*night frogs chant polyrhythms,*
and other things that might make you smile
if you come across it blown into a ditch or,
soggy, collapsed against a telephone pole:

if you like it, you can keep it
a love note from nature via
my odd shorthand

or just have a good soak in those
generous miracles (they have already
laid down a tattoo on the skin of my soul)

and, by leaving, pass them on

## Spring break, Quadra Island

That morning, the juice
of an orange and licorice tea
(mixed up with
moss, cold, loneliness, and the dangerous
sensation of having, for once, nothing to do)
obliged me to think deeply.
And so I sat and set about, again,
pinpointing what and who I am.

I was, in the end, not sure, and I like to be sure
of things.

But I did see that, daily,
in uncertainty, I seek forgiveness
from myself, timidly, for being human
such a mess of water, love, grief, blood
and unpredictable music
all of which (disguises removed)
mean, I think, life.

## there are still birds here

we are fortunate, and even
the ditch streams flow cheerful and clear

do you ever hear running water
with none nearby?
any number of explanations
could satisfy: a winter wren,
a hidden spring,
the wish to run away
pumping just behind your eyes

it doesn't follow, but it happens,
like unformed words or unhatched birds, an accidental
enharmonic shift, or like tears when
there are still birds here

## Oceansong

I have stalked this ocean moonpath
from seas Salish to Caribbean and back,
have tried countless times
to walk it: I sink, sink,
I sink again.

One day I swear I'll walk it yet,
most likely while she's on her way to set;
you can come with me if you like.
Your hand will be in mine, there will
be conch shells, each ear
a nautilus, tendrils listening for west,
the ripples our footholds,
tucked into the tides,
each swell a soft bank on which to lie
and dream new ways to harmonize.

# Earthsong

we everyday hear the birds
singing close by:
what about they who call
from far away and echo?
send your ears further:
that music can admit one
into magic.

I went out this morning
at quarter past six
(because of the birds)
it was still dark, and
I heard so many things
I can't tell you
but I'll try:

robins, leaves,
chickadees still insisting
*spring soon*, geese,
frogs, a single gentle note
from chimes (twice), a raven
and finally rain.
this honour: to be
outdoors when the rain begins
all at once but quietly as
a child who takes your hand
or a lover who lets go
safe.

I let the chickens out, go inside
myself (to where it
smells of sweet incense)
to make soft peach muffins,
eat pomegranate over the sink, crumble
garden lemon balm into tea
and isn't Earth an amazing joy?

I tune other sounds out
that I may hear her breathe in
between phrases.

## This little light

I sat in the springdusk woods tonight
while robins-on-all-sides faded
      to occasional owl, smoothly
while the darkening of the air smelled as
      churches did (old wood, musty books and mystery)
before the scent of their festering
      danger made its way to me
when I saw dark-in-light's-clothing
find a foothold in
      god with a capital He.

The sun sets sooner, and more quickly, here.

And I informed the gathering night and church:
there is a not insignificant light
inside me, and I am shining it
on my own terms.

## Ar Hyd y Nos

there is much I cannot know: her mother's lullabies,
the scent of the evening she knew she was in love,
the curtain colours on the kitchen windows of her life.
the space from my beginning to her end
was long, but these seem never long enough.

hand in the water, it's almost dark,
send out my pulse: out of the basin,
around the bend, across the strait, hit the ground
and up the hill to that bed
that is in two worlds:
my blood, say hello to my blood,
say goodbye.
hear the frogs cry, all through the night.

go on, go on
to the place of rest,
go straight to the place of rest.

## to think of a tree

                              I like to think of a tree as
                           unconcerned with perfection or,
                                        even, goodness,
                              to imagine it focused solely on
                                    wholeness, on green,
                                         on, I like to think,
                                                  love,
              the sense of love that means simply standing, taking sun and
                                            rain into yourself
                              and what flows out of you then is
                    what your gift is, for others, what is needed.

consider the dogwood:
it occurs to me now, leaf babies,
        that you do not return every spring, a thought
        I have lazily inherited: you are a generation untried,
        callow, and the old ones
        cannot come back to help.
in you, a whole fresh winter's rot
        and quiet have combined
and maybe your foreleaves, perhaps dead pieces of
        neighbours and friends nearby and distant kin and a host
        of hypogeal providers have made you who you are

                    new and alive and taking
                 for granted that you have the right
                to be here, to be fed, to be green.

## it must have been the onions

>*can't you stay awake, I knew you'd do this*

today I ask someone if I am bossy
and they say (paraphrased)
what the hell, you're
the opposite of bossy, you probably need
to be more bossy
>*don't deviate from the plan*

there was water in my eyes
it must have been the onions I was
chopping for the stuffing
>*don't ask for help*

it couldn't have been what he said
he said
>*I never said that*

yet his speech was of a tongue I couldn't learn,
he the judge of a trial I'd never win
>*that is a false accusation*

my hair was turning grey, becoming lighter
still I was too heavy to fly
>*I won't trust you anymore*

nevertheless I saw birds and decided to be one
I could eat little. my bones grew hollow
my flesh melted off, my feathers matted     I sang
and then I flew away
      *don't write, you might record things incorrectly*

a little thread of this remained
somewhere in a hidden pocket I forgot I had:
the right to have left, the right
to have any me left
      *don't tell, it isn't yours to tell*

and I'm fine now, I think
it must have been the onions.

## Commendation

On Sunday someone told me
they had picked their exit date,
and I can't forget the thought.

Perhaps I'm being selfish, but
I'll drink the dregs of forest time,
of ocean time,
whichever biome, island, sea;

I watch the sunrise from the woods,
the ray that first creeps in to touch the green,
acknowledge that I won't be here each dawn,
feel day's first cobweb on a human face,
see feather fall from flying goose to ground,
make gentle every footfall so I won't disturb the birds
and try without success to find the words.

## cheers

my deepest thanks
(written in heart's ink)
do not come with smiles,
which is just as well, since
they are mostly intended for
the Earth, who understands me
whether I am smiling or not.

winds from the east swirl the
water dreams inside me, the cup.
Earth keeps her bright windows open
and does not hide.

## born this way

here we go again: how
do I ever manage to
be anything but an animal
prickly and antsy,
tense but
puddling      unpredictable and contradictory, from the cold
      floor I
search wildly for something concrete
to pause me in
a spinning world—
      you, slight smudge of
unknown origin on the wall just above
the countertop      in the absence of anything
weightier, you'll do

please stop my mind from tilting
keep my pulse steady, smudge, by your
two dimensions remind me
that there are two ways to breathe and
it is necessary that they be alternated, no matter
what is happening in the remainder of one's body

better a little bit empty than
a little bit full
(my motto)
may get me into trouble, but I can
believe no other

my heart has squeezed too many
beats into the measure of my life so far,
so that I have stopped envying the birds.

## míqən

that night my firstborn had become
old enough to see a show
        downtown alone
and I wandered the park
  in spring, home too far
   to go to and return in the span
  of a one-long-act, no-intermission
dusk: I rested hard, that evening,
  on the moss-prickled
    oak meadow rockbed I chose, head
    down, eyes stone-closed, peacock
    cries notwithstanding.
when I did stand again,
  fresh life sat, regal,
   in my still-tired womb.

## sooner or later

if I keep silent,
will the world end sooner
or later?

we had thought hills were
eternal,
those dew-gentled stars of self-heal
in the grass,
the precious languages of birds
and certainly our gods. surely
water will last forever,
and beings who drink it:
humans, at least, if not ivory-billed woodpeckers or
western black rhinoceros or splendid poison frogs or

the planet, of course the planet, even
if we drain away
all life upon her? well

they may have been right, the one
who wrote that the greatest of these
is love: when there is no object
left for faith and no use hoping
('Mama, I'm thirsty'), in the end
I imagine some humans, then,
still loving,
in thirst and in hunger,

in sickness and in pain,
the air thin and the water sludge,
every tree brought low and the ground
cracked, tongue-parched,
waiting ('I don't want to die, Mama')

still loving to the end.
this ending-love is what
is all I believe in now.

# II. Summer

## In which there are at least four miracles at SELEK-TEL

    summer woods, today.
and I see a nymph
    for the first time—
    hair sun gold and
    skin bark brown, slipping
    behind moss. the songbirds ebullient
and the maples as canopies.
        such a gift

now it is raining in the sunny woods.
I can't explain it: there are no clouds above,
no wind to loose the drops of last night's shower
from the benevolent overstory but it rains,
off and on, here and there, and I listen

spider
        weaving a web
        in the sun between trees
I stop to watch.
        how interesting, I think, that
        they are weaving counterclockwise.
and then I laugh because,
    of course, it's clockwise
        from the other side

in its
    probably centuries of life
that cedar has never been touched
    by the sun precisely like this: that
    trickle of sap glistening     that
hollow between roots in shadow
this beam of light tracing
    the verdigrised bark at
        just that angle

and I am here to see it.

## water and I

water and I fall,
take turns pouring ourselves
into each other

every time I enter her
salt cold I think:
'why am I doing this again?
this was a whole lot easier in the Caribbean Sea'

and every time something floats
me onward—a brave woman,
a dead seal, the mosaic of stones
beneath my feet, finally the wish to at once fly
and be held

we use each other well
we pool, drip, splash and soak, and
she makes up most of who I am

## melon/begin

it's the tenth July,
and just now i popped
a knife edge into a melon
so ripe it actually
groaned as it split open juice-and-red
and i know the feeling, which
is not all bad

you began at my belly slowly warming, while
organs sidestepped gently and desire
had long since built a nameless nest
for you to land in and

begin, tiny seed and new
invisible
smaller than the little moths you are
afraid of in your bedroom now, and more helpless

i suppose we must have grown with every breath
until i ceased to grow and you commenced to breathe.
i remember waiting for the surprise of you to ripen,
there on our common vine, for
what seemed like quite some time.

## Brimming Moon Dream

I remember now,
   now that I look down
   into the sea:
it was swimming I dreamt of
   as I slept undermoon,
and her light grew brighter
   the longer I looked.
It pulsed a bit, or was that me?
Did the earth throb
   or my feet? They run over
   the ground like a cup
   that used to be mine but
I poured it out on purpose.

The wind is right about what
   might come
around the next curve of the clock or
the next corner of the calendar.
It would help if I could use, instead,
a sundial, yes,
and a moonstick, and be alone
most of the time.

The cool of the floor of the woods above
the cool even of

        water
over my head
as high as the moon.
I carry it inside me at the centre
  like the juicy stone of a fruit.

## Wilderness

We met in the wilderness
(I can't seem to speak their name).
I lift up my eyes to the Sooke Hills—

where does my help come from?
I help myself

to serving after serving
and lick my fingers one by one
with relish.

I have been criticized, not just once, for
licking a dish clean; but damn,
if you aren't licking out
your ice cream bowl,
I ask you,
are you really living
at all?

There has been a falling-out,
a finding out; having unearthed
an incompatibility
that could not be scaled
(compounded by isms and abuse)

    I am watchful,
      in case

there is a forest fire in me.

      Birds call
and I want to be Messiaen
   and I want to fly.

## light, and momentary troubles

*this is the way*
the way the salmonberry bird sings them into ripening
the way late sunlight slips down cedar boughs like slow honey
      from my golden fingers
the way to not get lost is to follow water
the way a quail runs!
the way to fit in: brush the forest from your skin
the way broom seedpods burst in August with a CRACK

*and the truth*
[this page left intentionally blank]
even sound is toxic now
it might get worse before it gets better

*and the life*      of river      of gnat
     of squirrel    of polypore    of owl
of cougar    of water strider    of cedar      of air
     of lichen    of salmon      of human
of sword fern    of murrelet    of bear      of soil
     depends on it

## the world gives me

the very sweetness of incense,
the crescent moon just there at the edge
of a black fir tree on a navy sky: a triadic
D-minor windchime with (oh my heart)
a second added; dry of bone, steam of tea,
tender conifer tips radiant green soft, soft
rose petals dried on a napkin and forgive me, but
I seem to be going around unplugging things again.

# ʔAdaits<u>x</u> in August 2021

night in a trench:
I learn what mosquito nets
are for, really learn.
walkie-talkie comms at all hours, grit
between my teeth.
this is where ants make their home,
who seem to resent somewhat my
subterranean intrusion;
I usually present to them as
vibrations alone, tonight
a giant solid overheated form tucked into
their refuge. just as a heat dome
came down and settled this summer.
cops walking by, flashlights in my eyes—'anyone there?'—
for 2, 3, 4 a.m. checks, no,
you can't fill this one in
(sorry not sorry)
right arm in a PVC pipe, chains
at the ready
and all I can think of
is the trees,
whom I love.

## unpolished

I had a manicure done once:
for my wedding, and you know
how that turned out: I ruined it
playing Schumann the night before
and had to have it redone
the next morning.

sweet morning after of life
free of polish, gods and spouses
here am I:
let us begin
again, again, and
again, naked and plain, opening
in a great swoop like Opus 17
and again, now ask me
again.

## tell me

speaking of the breeze: tell me!
      you must find in order
        to fall.
branches our bones, mossy, wands;
soft, in the end.
      find or fall
i have the healing inside me.
take your hunger
one leaf crackles
sink down inside the rock and
flow    (a soft dance)
disappear for a spell
and then cast it around yourself
      find, and fall.
now i listen,
careful about what goes inside.

## Arbutus

with your
ribbony skirts and
sly patches of bark on
skin smooth as silk.
so ineffective in terms of modesty,
so perfect in beauty.

## the echo of leaving

when he called me an adulteress,
the alders laughed in the dark. in my rage
I did not hear.
   it was truthful only in potentiality, such as:
if the wind had come
upon me alone,
who knows what might have happened?

can you see:
I must leave because
I cannot leave myself,
must trade for beauty
ashes
of the poems I never wrote
and spacious silence,
even if it's only a dream.

when will I be ready? when a thrush
takes my bent back for the land
   and rests fearless on my spine.
when there's no one but green air
around me, then trees,
the end as ancient and
       inevitable as sound.

the other night told me that
I don't need to change for the moon,
and it was my turn to laugh in the dark.

## Bike

this is the way the ladies ride, some of us, on
slim cracked shoulderless West Coast Road,
that is the curve and swoop
of the hilltops I see when I'm
on my way to find a refugium (away, away)
but now I think I understand:
we can't get there from here.

you are on the best route to your destination based
on current conditions, including but not limited to
washed-out roads, frequent fatal weather events,
Earth's flesh buckling as we lacerate her for oil,
mass extinction, garbage islands,
profit-driven development of what little green
is left, fires and floods, melting polar ice, clear-cut
mountains on all sides of town, and highways
blocked by necessary prophets abused
by keepers of the peace and impatient
commuters in vehicles that weigh
enough to kill an elk or a human.     I should tell you: yesterday,
for the first time in my life

I hit someone with my car, a squirrel,
I kill it. I hold it together for the others
and I never want to drive again.

where are we all going, and why so fast
and why so far?
I will pedal until my legs
are like stone, I will
pay the rain no mind (for nor
does it pay any to me)
pumping my
merry way up and gliding back,
politely turning down help and
side streets

for the hazard lights of
the planet have flicked on;
I can hear her gears grinding,
and our only home is between them

## All recycled materials

I always think I am going
    to the woods to untangle things,
stomp in with eyes on the root-earth-
        stone-leaf weave of the path
sit and mutter as I drop stitches into the creek
    or toss knots to the ground in
resignation

and, turning to leave,
    find that the needles
of hemlock and fir must have crept
   up beside me to knit my
  tatters into a gift of
        all recycled materials
for me
like me.

## god apology

I burned a bible last night. I'm not exactly
proud of it, but
    it needed doing and there I was,
  tending a fire, so

I apologized to god: nothing personal
                but
this has caused too much damage and

I doubt it was yours.
Of course, there is a way
    in which everything is—
but let this be
    my flickering exception.

# III. Autumn

## i, nemophile

my inner life includes
those melodies i hum
among the trees which
are not for human ears,
a stone settled in the crotch
of a rainslicked arbutus,
the way the ferns shiver when the wind
lets its barest
breath stroke the undersides of
their fronds, the come-hither
glitter
of sun-engorged droplets on hemlock—
who could resist?

(closing my eyes, half-blinded
by the flashing in and out, dark and light:
taking nothing
somehow given everything)

and most of all
the way the moss, beginning low, inches higher and
higher up the trunk, trying to reach its peak—
what a relief that, after all, it is no sin
to love the forest.

**who**

who stops to mourn the car-smacked wren,
dead creatures upon verges rising
as cairns to air—
who gives to the wind to scatter their riches
(they were hers at the last, at the first)—
who walks the path and does the work of one
who is grateful still for the
always-presence of the lonely
magic that is, that finds, that forms:

what shall this one receive
(at the last, at the first),
though their blood be small rivers
and waterfalls salted,
but inexorable, sumptuous
oneness?
fear is not becoming
and the seeds are many, if we
let them be.

# Summerland

In late October I daydream that I reassure the leaves—
     who quake and shiver as I
  when I fear, at times—
for I have seen
  what happens after the fall.
The fall: when they worry that
     they must stop dancing.

I have seen it with
  my own eyes, I would tell them
   (if I could):
  leaves that land, at the effortless
end of their descent,
  on this stream,
who sway underwater

     differently, yes: pulsed by
 the current, caught by
  root or stick or
held light-tender on
 jutting stone or
 spike of branch—but dancing
 just as much as they
 danced in the sky.

Summerland?
      I hope not exclusively
when one cold raindrop comes to rest
   precisely between wool stitches
  and hangs, trembling
against my skin,
a tap on the shoulder to charm my attention

 down
   gently
  from where it had spiralled
back to the ground.

## Someday witch

It's a good thing my hair is
        bark brown, otherwise
   how would I hide in the woods,
  camouflage.
What if it were red, or blonde
and what about
   when it turns grey,
or white.
I will let it clump like moss and
        trail like usnea
  and be a witch of the woods
    if I am given so many years (which is
what I want to be when I grow up)
with a hood of sea mist,
        a shroud of fog.

# Windsong

Even I! (creeper of the forest floor) need to go up high
   at times
   above the trees
   so I can see the mountains
where the wind plays
      the holes of my body
   like a flute
under this chill
November drizzle
at PKOLS.

I laugh open fourths
with the wind, tune
myself to sing perfect
consecutive fifths
above its drone,
above its ground.

## Thirsty

When the world is this wet—
    soaking from and dripping on and filling,
    swishing over and churning past and covering—
  I am so thirsty that
  I drink and drink
and I wonder what
  I am trying to drown.

## In which the fish teach philosophy at SELEK̵TEL̵

I go to the stream
        to rinse my honeyed hands,
    come face to face with a
    coho face to face with death
resting in the shelter of a fallen cedar
    post-spawning: the end is near

I apologize aloud, change my mind,
back away; let my skin remain sticky
I will show my respect to the elders.

As the air I'm breathing
        is saturated with
    particles of fish, should
   it be called water? that which
I take in with this breath may once have been bubbles
    and if I did wash myself

in an autumn river full of salmon
making life and dying and decaying,
perhaps I would be cleaner than before.

## Ides of November

  One day may I
let my knees go
  to earth and spread
bow my head, find a
  safety-place of which
some say none remain, but
  I may find one yet
(eternal optimist), for
  hear this: I met a sister,
yesterday, I didn't
  know I had.

Corporeal life seems
  all, some days;
our blood defies gravity
  half the time.

On a journey overwater I saw
  how much reflections change
with weather, how much our
  swellings and heart tides
shift with the sky.

While the rivers
  flood and towns are
drowned, we sit
  in pain and safety,

fretting: organs that
  fail, savings that ebb,
memories that lose their grip,
  insecure passwords lacking
special characters, sleepless
  nights, and hunted wolves
and eagle rays.

  I see you, you who are tired
of this way and wish for that
  out-of-reach dream, that mirage of
a lifetime goal made unattainable by
  the whole world's greed
for belonging.

**peace**

I have not made my peace
with the hollowness of hegemony,
the amount of food required to stay alive,
the staleness of the air indoors when one has been without;
with toilets that flush clean water,
talk of buying ski chalets, or waking
not hemmed in by trees.
My peace, rather, is that which
they give unto me, not as
the world gives
but greener, and smelling of
sap and change.

## Shall I go?

I have believed and ceased believing many things
but if I were to believe no longer
   that the arbutus leaves in their
  rustling were speaking to me
then how could I go on?

  Progress, they say.
There isn't room enough for all of us here.
  Shall I go?

  I feel it keenly in my bones
   I stop and stand and write mid-hill
as if in the last
   moment of my life
  I hear something like windchimes
  (my angelic trumpet)

but the geese, I think, have
        no words for north or south.

## getting somewhere

the high-flying geese and I are getting somewhere today,
they probably someplace warmer, I
only racing the sharp rain to the grocery store on
my bike for foods to tempt
sick children, tucked each into a bed
  all under the same splattering, shining dark
sunny bank of late November cloud
barely skirting Sooke to the south,
all under
the same sky

I think as I ride: our world has filled, has changed,
and no room remains now
for any more
hate

# Hedgerow

*for Jan Zwicky*

The best place in this house
(and at least one other I know, and likely more)
is out between siding and cedar hedge,
that sliver of space where I can creep,
and do, from which to stare cold and unseen
at the trees in their gold half-sungowns.
How is it that the ones behind are lit,
while those in front are not? as the chambers of my heart
when nightmares are stacked yet in the mail
come poems.

## Air

Air that fills the spaces:
between leaves on that chestnut,
between bee and its comb, air in
my mouth even when it is closed,
between pen and paper at the ends
of words, in bubbles of fish
and in bones of birds. Air in my
woodstove keeps me warm. Air in a
concert hall, vibrating madly; air in a
coffin. A cello. A lightbulb. Must
there not be air in the right places,
and not the wrong, like veins and vaginas,
syringes, guts. We want our air clean,
just right, enough.

## G.P.

you always wonder: when will the rains come?
when will the moon come?
when will the geese, the dark,
the apples, salmon, or the end come?

when will knowing come, or surety?

much as I'd like a nice five-one
    (in root position, timpani and all)
I suspect reality
is much more atonality
    or fade, or a grand pause

and quiet forgetting
to come in again.

# IV. Winter

## Doorway

There is an unlit door in me,
I see it when my eyes are closed;
it's mine alone. On each approach
I grow and heighten, stretch and warm,
with magic in my limbs,
and the world and I switch places:
I the outside, she within.
A dark, dark doorway built
of voice, bone, skin.

## Owlmas

I'm nearing forty. There is still
something comforting in sleeping
on the couch on a winter night in
the mild glow of a lit tree,
though I hold faith no longer
in a christ or any kind of mass,
having relocated to a state
of mind where one puts faith in
planting garlic with the neighbours,
in fire, in the wisdom of bodies,
in the calling of the great horned owls
who duet across my house each
December: alto from the east,
tenor to the west.
And you might like to know
that I have never been homesick.

# Windows

I have thought much on windows,
and much of them. Just as we burn
small lights at night to hold the dark away
because we fear its kiss, we build as well our
walls on every side, and roof, and floor—
but know enough of love, and maybe bliss, to
leave or knock or carve out space for space, for precious joining
      space of out and in.

And I have learned of nightlights
their other, better purpose: when a child
is sick, or fretful, or myself, unsleeping thanks
to language running through my soul, we
might work through what is needed with as little glow,
as much darkness near and patient, as can be.
My breath, when I am inside, still seeks the windows,
      for both out and in.

## *Another storm comin'*

I am in the woods this morning when
all at once it is darker and
trees begin to creak ominously
   the whoosh and susurration
  sing high, seep
down to where I
stand, successfully reminded of
the gossip I heard in town
   yesterday and promptly forgot:
  *Another storm comin'.*

I see raindrops striking puddles
   before I feel them begin
     to strike me.

## Drawn

    A new start is coming—but

might I dovetail it
    blend it with seawater, blurring
   the edges while melding
     past, present and
   future selves in one cauldron
hung warm over flames of
 shifting changing
  renewal,
modulate so gingerly that
both tonics ring true

or does a start mean also
    of necessity
      an end?

## December medicine

I am stopped in my
        proverbial and literal tracks on the
   fifth-shortest day of the year
   by the way the sunlight hits the west
   sides of the mild grey alder trunks and
my favourite colour is grey today.

Some mornings I don't stop to
  put anything on my feet because
I wish I'd been out of doors
     before I even woke up
and I gulp the cool air like I'm
  drinking down
 a blue medicine that will
heal all the things unhealed.

I breathe in the same air into which
      raven has cried,
        and eagle.

Look:
  for it is all
  a miracle
  out there.

## Odd

the midwives neglected to tell me this part: how
ten years postpartum
my chest would thrum, my milk trickle down
when I see snowy firs
or rocks in the creek, or read a poem or
hear a fugue

i suppose i must want
to feed the whole world.

# Lines on the shortest day

There is something about that loop,
that link, that I slept
within her womb a speck,
expelled by the power
of the mother between, and she within
her mother's mother's too, and on.
As it happens,
she told us in November of her ninety-eighth year
that her mother had
come to call, whereupon
my own womb breathed small
knowing up my spine: soon. How close
is wisdom to what they call senility;
of the same seed.
I had somehow known at Samhain
that she would grace next year's altar, be included when
next I riffle through my years for still shots
of aunt to cancer, grandmother to pneumonia, friend found
dead in a Mexican hotel room     and I will
place flowers there, will plant them
deep in summer so they are born
at dark autumn's bloom.

## Gardening in January

There was frost, at dawn, and the air wasn't sure
    if it was misty or clear
but after a while I went out anyway
    to dig and to clip.
Oh old dry shoots of orach and mugwort, sage and self-heal, you
are brittle, hollow
and as always, the blackberries assume
control of all.
But let us let go
go underground, you and I, and emerge
    in a few months
with more ease, and secure in the knowledge
that the dirt is home.

## Point No Point

whenever I pass Point No Point I
remember a couple I once knew
who went for an anniversary trip there
every year until one of them perhaps
grew into me or maybe even more so and the other
perhaps stayed the same or maybe even more so and
sometimes there really is
no point

## thy neighbour's chimes

I haven't walked this way before,
but now I will again: a whole
fresh symphony of rhythm,
tempo, colour, tone,
in wood or silver cylinder or
hollow churchbell gonging—
bells, the best part of
churches now—
which hand hung them there,
just so? where air sips
modes from metal, never the same
song twice
quite, or if so
you're struck dumb, wondering.

## The waiting-time

Be still under
this great sharp sky,
fresh sky of longing against patience, contrast
of black
branch on pale canvas
simultaneous
like harmony or evening,
like breath and thought,
pain and freedom.

Let wonder be
and pour life into
the waiting-time,
but taste too the melting
flakes of anticipation
(sweet and ethereal) in the moments
when they overflow, sudden,
vulnerable, onto your tongue.

## Magellan Quay

you warm bright jungle, of
shades so dense you green the eye,
saturate the soul of those
who behold you in sunshine—
open-hearted, at night I walk your dark
and silvered corridor from sea to moon,
alone;
you shift, and I with you.
night, the tale-weaver:
fill yourself
from her stores, you cannot
deplete them

   though tonight the moon wanes nearly half, and I
will not see her face before I sleep.
you are vanishing day by day, thinning
and vanishing
   and the moon will return
and you, deep green, will not.

## It is February

and tears come to my eyes
because I won't hear a
Swainson's thrush for weeks
or months yet,
in the dappled golden deep
moss green of slow summer
woods, and
I need to hear it now.

**once was lost**

to search I went outside
for a missing earring, a happy
misunderstanding, as it lay waiting
on the bathroom counter, but I'm
glad I did, for a small piece
of my soul sat by the woodpile
in the sun, which I did not
know was lost.

## Remembering blue

I admit it: I
forgot, again, this
grey slate slick winter,
about the colour of the ocean
so that when I came
around a corner this morning and
saw it under the sun
deep, royal cobalt I laughed
aloud to myself, 'It's blue, blue!
The ocean is *blue!*'

I am not sorry about forgetting
because it gives me a chance
(every spring)
to remember
again.